The author reserves all rights to this book. They do not permit anyone to reproduce or transmit any part of this book through any means or form be it electronic or mechanical. No one also has the right to store the information herein in a retrieval system, neither do they have the right to photocopy, record copies, scan parts of this document, etc., without the proper written permission of the publisher or author.

Copyright © 2022 Williams Books
All Rights Reserved

By Laura Williams
Translated by Zainab Shah

© 2022 Williams Books
1 rue de l'église, 91430 Igny
Dépôt légal : Décembre 2022
ISBN 978-2-494614-59-8
Imprimé à la demande par Amazon
Loi n° 49-956 du 16 juillet 1949 sur les publications destinées à la jeunesse

سيب

[saib] – apple

مگرناشپاتی

[magar nashpati] - avocado

کیلا

[kela] – banana

پھلیاں

[phalyaan] - beans

گوبھی

[gobhi] - cabbage

گاجر

[gajar] - carrot

مرچ

[mirch] – chilli

مكئى

[makai] – corn

كھیرا

[kheera] – cucumber

بینگن

[baingan] - eggplant

لهسن

[lehsan] – garlic

ادرک

[adrak] – ginger

سبز پھلیاں

[sabz phalyaan] - green beans

امرود

[amrood] – guava

ليمون

[leemon] – lemon

آم

[aam] - mango

كُھمبی

[khumbi] - mushroom

پیاز

[pyaz] – onion

كينو

[keenu] – orange

پپیتا

[papeeta] - papaya

گُلِ صلیبی

[gul-e-salibi] – passion fruit

مونگ پھلی

[moong phalli] - peanut

مٹر

[matar] – peas

اناناس

[annanaas] – pineapple

آلو

[aalu] – potato

لوکی

[loki] – pumpkin

چاول

[chawal] - rice

سويا

[soya] - soy

پالک

[palak] – spinach

گَنّا

[ganna] - sugar cane

شكر قندى

[shakar kandi] - sweet potato

ٹماٹر

[tamatar] - tomato

تربوز

[tarbooz] – watermelon

گندم

[gandum] - wheat

Thank you

Thank you for purchasing "Urdu-English Words for Toddlers"! Your support means a lot to me, and I hope you and your child enjoy these books.

If you have a moment, I would greatly appreciate it if you could leave a review on Amazon. Your feedback will help me improve future editions of the series and create more resources for bilingual children.

Thank you again for your support. You can access the reviews on Amazon by scanning the QR code below or by visiting the link below:

https://www.amazon.com/review/create-review?&asin=2494614597

Thank you for helping me continue my work as a language teacher and translator. Your support is greatly appreciated!

In the same collection

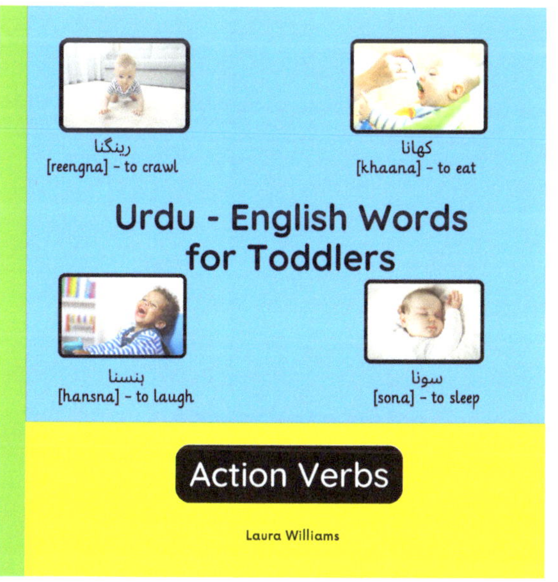

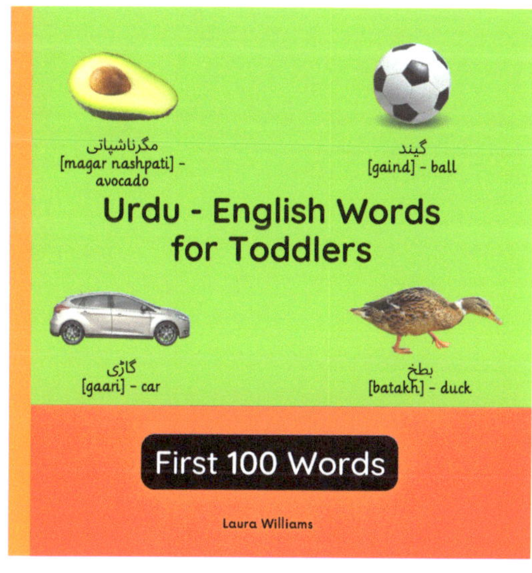

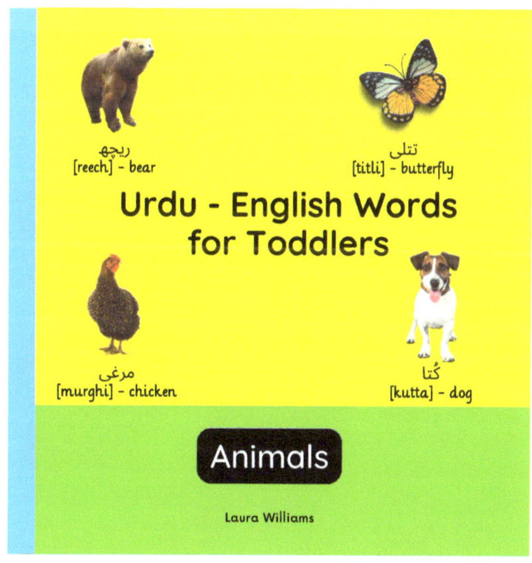

www.ingramcontent.com/pod-product-compliance
Lightning Source LLC
LaVergne TN
LVHW071655180726
843512LV00002B/459